Some Things I Said

DAVID FERRY

Some Things I Said

Editors
Elizabeth Ferry, Stephen Ferry, George Kalogeris

Poetry
David Ferry

Photography
Stephen Ferry

Typographic Design Concept and Design
Diego Amaral / Amaral Editores SAS

Cover Design
Stephen Ferry, Victoria Sarria

Printing
Panamericana Formas e Impresos S.A.

ISBN: 979-8-218-26770-4

First edition: November 2023

Impreso en Colombia
Printed in Colombia

GROLIER SERIES OF ESTABLISHED POETS
Grolier Poetry Book Shop
6 Plympton Street
Cambridge, MA 02138
www.grolierpoetrybookshop.org

This work is dedicated
to the memory of my wife,
Anne Davidson Ferry.

CONTENTS

INTRODUCTION

Here is an entirely unique book, the only one of its kind that I know to exist: an anthology of the works excerpted and brilliantly transformed into the single weave of one of David Ferry's most beautiful poems, "Some Things I Said."

Whatever else David Ferry's poem is, it is first an elegy for Anne Ferry, whose own brilliant scholarship helps us read and understand "Some Things I Said." In *Tradition and the Individual Poem*, Anne Ferry reminds us that the "Greek root for anthology—anthos (flower) + legein (to gather)—was still fully alive in the second half of the eighteenth century."

In Roman literature and myth, "gathering flowers" is a potentially dangerous, even a lethal, activity. Eurydice was engaging in this childlike action, almost the insignium of innocence and guilelessness, when the serpent bit her. "I said death lives in our words," David Ferry writes, as though to scold himself for failing to heed his own warning.

But: was it a warning, or a boast? Death lives in our words; it carries on, survives us, feeds the harvest downstream. You see this principle enacted in the strongly broken yet strongly bonded chain that forms this poem. Chronology is upended; the old words "are modified," as Auden reminds us, "in the guts of the living."

In the two consecutive sections of the poem connected by the strongest syntactic bond, the first passage is "new"—written for this poem—while the second, which supersedes it, is "old"—a summary of some lines from David Ferry's own translation of Book VII of *The Aeneid*:

Right there before my eyes was the one who said
where are you now? Where
are you Anne? I was the one

*

Who saw how Aeneas lay there in the darkness watching the light, the little motions of light moving around the ceiling and telling him something

But really everything here is new, since it occupies space not in the sphere of writing but in the zone of saying: the risky performance made by a living body in unfolding time. David Ferry and I were educated by the same schools and according to the same principles, several generations apart. In those Robert Frost-obsessed classrooms, we both learned that speech is primary, that writing does its best to capture its magic but cannot but fail.

"Some Things I Said": the emphasis is everything. "Some Things I Said": the "I" that speaks the poem is not a silo of identity; it is perforated, porous, made from the things it hears or overhears.

"Some Things I Said." No big deal: not touchstones, not clarifications of life. We use the phrase "just something I said" to mean I've moved on, I've said other things since. Stanley Cavell's great title comes to mind: *Must We Mean What We Say?*

And, by the way, to think about the title to the poem as I do, above, is again to mark a debt to Anne Ferry, whose study *The Title to the Poem* changed the way many people read poems: poems in their entirety, poems all the way through, not merely their titles.

*

Since we're in the realm of self-quotation, I wanted to quote some paragraphs I wrote for a clandestine occasion: a reader's report prepared for the University of Chicago on the manuscript of David Ferry's translation of Virgil's *Aeneid*. I have tried to think of ways, over the years, to bring them to light, because I think they describe Ferry's accomplishment accurately.

They especially apply to "Some Things I Said," and its fascinating relationship to syntactic rupture and to syntactic repair. My self-quotation here embeds a quotation from Ferry's Virgil: who is the "I" who said these things? *Tradition and the Individual Poem*, indeed.

Ferry's syntax, learned from Wordsworth but perfected as a supple and muscular American style over the course of his unparalleled career, is perfectly matched to Virgil's poem. I will quote only one example, and without reference to the Latin (I am not a classicist, though I can read Latin reasonably well and have myself translated some of the famous bits of the poem). This is from Book II, when Aeneas is recapping his trials for Dido, describing the appearance of Pyrrhus in battle:

There in the vestibule of the royal palace,
And at the very doors, there's exultant Pyrrhus,
Shining in the glitter of his armor;
It's as when winter's cold is over and
A serpent having nourished his poisons on
The underground herbs he ate while he lay waiting
All winter long for spring to make its return,
Comes forth and sheds his skin, and he's youthful again,
Youthful and shining, his old skin sloughed away,
His crest erect, his menacing breast held high,
His fluent body wreathing and coiling, ready.

The art here is astounding, especially the way that single sentence, moving through the simile of the snake's skin and imperceptibly back to the body of Pyrrhus, comes to rest on the single word: "ready." And the music of that repetition of the word "youthful," the second occurrence augmented with a second adjective, "shining," expressing the wonder of his appearance: I'm amazed by that moment, just as Aeneas is amazed in describing it. Ferry's own amazement is clear as he beholds the beauty, the readiness, the ferocity of the man, remade in the moment of battle.

Those were some things I said after closing the book on one of the great reading experiences of my life. Inwardly transformed though outwardly munching a Goldfish cracker in an airplane high above the Atlantic Ocean, I might have asked myself the question Ferry, quoting his own "At a Bar," asks at the close of this strange and beautiful poem: "What is my name and nature?"

—DAN CHIASSON

Some Things I Said

writings on the wall

*

I was the one who said
the ditch in the backyard was maybe a river
that had flowed from somewhere else and was flowing to
somewhere else

*

I was the one who said where are you now?

*

I was the one who told about the one whose photograph in
the book of Eakins's photographs was of
a guy the perfection of his body was his doom, and
Shakespeare said so too

*

Right there before my eyes was the one who said
where are you now? Where
are you Anne? I was the one

*

Who saw how Aeneas lay there in the darkness watching the
light, the little motions of light moving around the ceiling
and telling him something

*

I was the one whose mother's voice called out of the urn
beseeching

*

I was the one who said how the day light knocks at the lid in
vain

*

I said be keep to your self be close be wall all dark

*

I said good people are punished, like all the rest

*

I said the boats on the river are taking it easy

*

I said the brain in your head whispers

*

I said death lives in our words

*

I said how beautiful is the past, how few the implements,
and how carefully made

*

I was the one who said
her body witness is, so also is her voice

*

I said better not know too much too soon all about it

*

where rhymes with beware, I said

*

I said it is the body breathing,
the crib of knowing

*

I wish I could recall now the lines written across my dream is what
I said

*

I said the horse's hooves know all about it, the sky's statement of
oncoming darkness

*

The fumes on the roof are visible and drifting away like
martyred souls, I said

*

I said the knees of the committee touch each other under the
table, furtive in pleasure

*

I said
Eurydice, My Father

*

I said we huddle over the ice,
the two of us

*

To squeeze from a stone its juice is her art's happiness is
what I said

*

I am the one who said,
I hum to myself myself in a humming dream

*

And how we're caught, I said,
In language: in being, in feeling, in acting. I said, it's
exacting

*

I said the sea upheld us, would not let us go nor drown us,
and we looked down say a million years, and there were the
fish

*

See, the dead bloom in the dark, I said

*

The nightjar feeds while flying softly, smiling, smiling, I said

*

I said revenant whitefaced Death is walking not knowing
whether

*

I said the formula on the blackboard said who are you

*

I said Utnapishtim said to Gilgamesh blink of an eye

*

I said where are you now   Where are you Anne

*

Stanza my stone my father poet said

*

vwx   stones and sticks

*

The day doesn't know what day it is, I said

*

What's in the way the sun shines down, I said

*

I cried in my mute heart,
What is my name and nature

Some Things

I Said

Everybody's Tree

The storm broke over us on a summer night,
All brilliance and display; and being out,
Dangerously I thought, on the front porch standing,
Over my head the lightning skated and blistered
And sizzled and skidded and yelled in the bursting down
Around my maybe fourteen-years-old being,
And in spite of all the fireworks up above
And what you'd thought would have been the heat of all
That exuberant rage, the air was suddenly cool
And fresh and as peaceable as could be,
Down on the porch, so different from what it was
My body was expecting. The raindrops on
The front porch railing arms peacefully dripped
As if they weren't experiencing what
Was coming down from above them as an outrage.
My body could reinterpret it as a blessing,
Being down there in the cool beneath the heat.
It wasn't of course being blessed but being suddenly
Singled out with a sense of being a being.

Sometime early on in the nineteenth century,
Down in the part of New Jersey called New Sweden,
Someone with some familial link to me,
Maybe a grandsire down a maternal line,
Whose name was Isaiah Toy, was sitting up
In the house of his dying bachelor uncle, who
Was also Isaiah Toy, and Isaiah Toy,
His uncle, would leave his farm to Isaiah Toy,
His nephew, who was sitting in a chair
In the next room to where his uncle was dying.
I don't know what kind of light it would have been
That he was reading the Bible by while his uncle
Slept toward leaving the farm to him, when suddenly,
Reading, who was it, Matthew, or maybe Mark,
The glory of the Lord broke over his head,
Or so he said. Methodists got excited when
In the woods of their confusion suddenly
The moonlight burst above their heads and they
Were ever after then enlightened beings.
"Light suddenly broke upon his mind. For fear
Of disturbing his dying uncle with his joy,
The expression of which he could not repress, he went

I was the one who said
the ditch in the backyard was maybe a river
that had flowed from somewhere else and was flowing to
somewhere else

Out of the house into the brilliant moonlight
Shining upon the snow, and gave vent to his feelings,
Shouting 'Glory to God! Glory to God in the Highest.'"

Coming back in from the porch, while the storm went on
Above our little house, I went to close the window
Of the dining room that looked out back of the house
And I could see, could dimly see, the backs
Of the Bowdoin Street houses all in a row,
Occasionally lit up and washed blank by
Downpours of the lightning of the storm:
The Beckers' house, the Gileses' house, the Demarests',
Jean Williams's where she lay in "the sleeping-sickness."
And Bessie Phelps's house, the one next to hers,
The property lines of the houses and their yards
Made briefly briefly clear by the lightning flashing.
Running along the back of the hither yards
Was a tiny ditch defining the property lines
Between where our Yale Street backyards ended
And where the yonder Bowdoin Street houses' backyards
Backed up to it; my childhood fantasy thought
The waterless tiny ditch was the vestige of
A mysterious long ago bygone vanished river
That came from somewhere else and went somewhere.
I don't know, didn't know, though of course I knew them,
Whatever went on in those houses, or in my mind,
Or my mother's mind, or my father's, asleep upstairs,
Though I kept wondering, and wonder still,
What is it they were doing? Who were they?
All, all, are gone, the unfamiliar faces.

Over beyond in the night there was a houseless
Wooded lot next door to Bessie's house;
Because of the houselessness and because of the trees,
I could think of it as a forest like the forest
In Hawthorne's great short story "Young Goodman Brown,"
And from out that window looking out at the back
I could faintly see, or thought I could see,
Maybe once or twice, by a flash, a raining gust
Of the light of lightning, the waving tops of trees
In that empty wooded lot beyond Bessie's house.
The houseless tiny lot seemed like a forest
And in the forest there was a certain tree
Which all of us children somehow knew was known

*

As Everybody's Tree, so it was called,
Though nobody knew who it was who gave it its name;
And on the smooth hide of its trunk there were initials,
Nobody knew who it was who had inscribed them.
We children had never gathered around that tree
To show each other our bodies.
I remember how
Crossing through that houseless wooded lot,
On my way home on an autumn afternoon,
That strange tree, with the writing on it, seemed
Ancient, a totem, a rhapsody playing a music
Written according to an inscrutable key.
How did I ever know what the tree was called?
Somebody must have told me. I can't remember.
Whoever it was has become a shade imagined
From an ancient unrecoverable past.

*

Soul

What am I doing inside this old man's body?
I feel like I'm the insides of a lobster,
All thought, and all digestion, and pornographic
Inquiry, and getting about, and bewilderment,
And fear, avoidance of trouble, belief in what,
God knows, vague memories of friends, and what
They said last night, and seeing, outside of myself,
From here inside myself, my waving claws
Inconsequential, wavering, and my feelers
Preternatural, trembling, with their amazing
Troubling sensitivity to threat;
And I'm aware of and embarrassed by my ways
Of getting around, and my protective shell.
Where is it that she I loved has gone to, as
This cold sea water's washing over my back?

I was the one who said where are you now?

Photographs from a Book

I

A poem again, of several parts, each having to do
With a photograph. The first, by Eakins, is of his student,
Samuel C. Murray, about twenty-five years old,

Naked, a life study, in the cold light and hungry
Shadow of Eakins's studio in Philadelphia.
The picture was taken in eighteen ninety-two.

The young man's face is unsmiling, shy, or appears to be so
Because of the shadow. One knows from other
Images in the book that Murray's unshadowed gaze

Can look out clear, untroubled, without mystery or guile.
His body is easy in its selfhood, in its self and strength;
The virtue of its perfection is only of its moment

In the light and shadow. In the stillness of the photograph
I cannot see the light and shadow moving
As light and shadow move in the moving of a river.

I was the one who told about the one whose photograph in
the book of Eakins's photographs was of
a guy the perfection of his body was his doom, and
Shakespeare said so too

That Now Are Wild and Do Not Remember

Where did you go to, when you went away?
It is as if you step by step were going
Someplace elsewhere into some other range
Of speaking, that I had no gift for speaking,
Knowing nothing of the language of that place
To which you went with naked foot at night
Into the wilderness there elsewhere in the bed,
Elsewhere somewhere in the house beyond my seeking.
I have been so dislanguaged by what happened
I cannot speak the words that somewhere you
Maybe were speaking to others where you went.
Maybe they talk together where they are,
Restlessly wandering, along the shore,
Waiting for a way to cross the river.

Right there before my eyes was the one who said
where are you now? Where
are you Anne? I was the one

VIRGIL

The Aeneid (Book VIII, lines 27-41)

That's how it was in Latium. And while all this
Was happening, the hero, Laomedon's heir,
Was all at sea in his mind about what to do,
Thinking about the war and what it is,
What was the plan, what were the dangers, how
Was it to go, thinking about these things
Over and over, looking this way and that,
As when the light on the trembling surface of water,
In a bronze bowl in a room, in the dark, reflecting
Perhaps the light of a ray of sunlight, or
Maybe a ray of moonlight coming in
Through a window of the room, is fleetingly seen
To touch and show itself on this or that object,
Or else on this or that place on the walls of the room,
And sometimes high above on the ceiling panels.

Who saw how Aeneas lay there in the darkness watching the
light, the little motions of light moving around the ceiling
and telling him something

Rereading Old Writing

Looking back, the language scribbles.
What's hidden, having been said?
Almost everything? Thrilling to think
There was a secret there somewhere,
A bird singing in the heart's forest.

Two people sitting by a river;
Sunlight, shadow, some pretty trees;
Death dappling in the flowing water;
Beautiful to think about,
Romance inscrutable as music.

Out of the ground, in New Jersey, my mother's
Voice, toneless, wailing–beseeching?
Crying out nothing? A winter vapor,
Out of the urn, rising in the yellow
Air, an ashy smear on the page.

The quiet room floats on the waters,
Buoyed up gently on the daylight;
The branch I can see stirs a little;
Nothing to think about; writing
Is a way of being happy.

What's going to be in this place?
A person entering a room?
Saying something? Signaling?
Writing a formula on a blackboard.
Something not to be understood.

I was the one whose mother's voice called out of the urn
beseeching

A Farewell

Let the day fall like light out of the eye.
Out of the ear let its music go. From the touch
Let the touching of air retire. Remain in the dark,
Dumbly remain in the dark. What will they know
Of you then, or want, when, then, in the dark you remain?

Knowledge began with the pressure of light on the eye,
And the ear spun out of thin air its airy tune.
Let no vein flutter or flicker to signal the blood's
All but imperceptible errand. Does the skin
Shudder or shiver at all at least conjunction?

Shrink, then, into your dark, be locked up in yourself,
Shadow of shadow be in your nothing dark,
Oh be keep to yourself, be close, be moat, be wall
All dark. Hush. Hear hush. Vanish. Know nothing.
How then will the day light knock at the lid in vain!

I was the one who said how the day light knocks at the lid in
vain

A Farewell

Let the day fall like light out of the eye.
Out of the ear let its music go. From the touch
Let the touching of air retire. Remain in the dark,
Dumbly remain in the dark. What will they know
Of you then, or want, when, then, in the dark you remain?

Knowledge began with the pressure of light on the eye,
And the ear spun out of thin air its airy tune.
Let no vein flutter or flicker to signal the blood's
All but imperceptible errand. Does the skin
Shudder or shiver at all at least conjunction?

Shrink, then, into your dark, be locked up in yourself,
Shadow of shadow be in your nothing dark,
Oh be keep to yourself, be close, be moat, be wall
All dark. Hush. Hear hush. Vanish. Know nothing.
How then will the day light knock at the lid in vain!

I said be keep to your self be close be wall all dark

To Sally

Now we've been sitting up all night,
Waiting to find out
What the story is.

I watch your beautiful patient face;
It's as if you didn't know
All that you know.

Your mother in mortal danger, you speak
Of something funny that happened.
What will have happened,

Maybe, before your story's finished?
Good people are punished
Like all the rest.

I said good people are punished, like all the rest

Down by the River

The page is green. Like water words are drifting
Across the notebook page on a day in June
Of irresistible good weather. Everything's easy.

On this side of the river, on a bench near the water,
A young man is peaceably stroking the arm of a girl.
He is dreaming of eating a peach. Somebody's rowing,

Somebody's running over the bridge that goes over
The highway beyond the river. The river is blue,
The river is moving along, taking it easy.

A breeze has come up, and somewhere a dog is barking,
Acknowledging the stirring of the breeze.
Nobody knows whose dog. The river is moving,

The boats are moving with it or else against it.
People beside the river are watching the boats.
Along the pathway on this side of the river

Somebody's running, looking good in the sunshine,
Everything going along with everything else,
Moving along in participial rhythm,

Flowing, enjoying, taking its own sweet time.
On the other side of the river somebody else,
A man or a woman, is painting the scene I'm part of.

A brilliantly clear diminutive figure works
At a tiny easel, and as a result my soul
Lives on forever in somebody's heavenly picture.

I said the boats on the river are taking it easy

Poem

The mind's whispering to itself is its necessity
To be itself and not to be any other,
If only for the moment as it passes.
It eats what it needs from the world around itself.
Slowly it makes its way floating through temperatures,
Degrees and other degrees of light and dark.
It moves through all things by virtue of its own
Characteristics. Mainly it is silent.
But when it utters a sound it is a sound
That others find hard to interpret, and that's known,
It supposes, only to another creature
It dreams of, so similar to itself as not
To have an entirely separate identity.
Somewhere there may be such a creature.
Emerson said: "They may be real; perhaps they are."
Yet it also thinks it's the only one, and is lonely.
It can be silent and unknown except
To itself or not even known to itself for long
Periods of time in sleepless reverie.
It is never asleep during the long nights of sleep.

I said the brain in your head whispers

News from Mount Amiata

– Montale

By later tonight the fireworks of the storm
Will be a swarming of bees below the horizon.
I'm writing this letter to you at a wooden table
Whose wood the insects and worms have gotten into.
The beams are pockmarked with their ravenous feasting.
A smell of melon mildew rises from the floor,
As from the valley rises the valley smoke,
As it were the smoke of mushrooms, clouding my window.
Here in the rich core of the world, in this room,
In this honeycomb, mealy, fragrant, innermost cell
Of a sphere launched out across the luminous skies,
You who are elsewhere and other dwell in another
Cell and center of things, but, here at this table,
Writing to you, in front of this fire the chestnuts
Lavishly burst themselves open upon the hearth of,
That life is too brief that invokes your absent presence
Against the glowing background as of an icon.

Outside the windows the rain is falling ...

If you
Were to make your way among the ancient feeble
Soot-blackened buildings time has made that way,
And along the alleys between them, and through the courtyards
Where in the middle there is a wellhead where
The well goes down forever and forever,
If you could follow the heavy flights of nightbirds
Down the alleys to where, beyond the ravine,
The galaxy glimmers, the matrix of our torment ...
But the only step that echoes along the darkness
Is that of someone by himself who sees
Shadows of doorways falling, shadows collapsing;
The threads between the stars are lost to sight;
The clock in the campanile is stopped at two;
Even the vines that climb the ancient walls
Are shadows that climb in the dark.

North Wind, come down,
Unloosen the hands that clutch the sandstone walls;
Scatter the books of hours on the attic floors.
Clear all away, cold wind, and then, let all

I said death lives in our words

Be clearness of sight that has dominion over
The mind that does not know how to despair.
Cold wind, seal up the spores from which the tendrils
Sprout that then climb as shadows the ancient walls.
These alleys are too narrow; the donkey hooves
That clatter in the darkness on the cobbles
Strike sparks the unseen mountain peak above
Replies to with magnesium random signals;
And oh the leaking slowly deliquescing
Walls of the huddled houses in the rain,
Time turning to water, the endless dialogue
With the wretched dead, the ashes, oh, the wind,
The death, the death that lives. ...

This Christian fuss—
Nothing but words of shadow and of grief—
What can I say through them that speaks to you?
Less than the water draining away down the runnels.
An old abandoned mill wheel, the trunk of a tree,
Markers of the limits of the world ...
A pile of litter shakes and disintegrates ...
At night the porcupines come out, seeking
A trickle of water to pity them ... They join
My waking vigil to your deep dreaming sleep.

*

Photographs from a Book

V

The Anasazi drink from underground rivers.
The petroglyph cries out in the silence of the rock
The tourist looks at. The past is beautiful.

How few the implements and how carefully made
The dwelling place, against the wind and heat.
Looking at a photograph, as at a petroglyph,

How little there is to go on. "The darkest objects
Reflect almost no light, or none at all,
Causing no changes in the salt in the emulsion."

In the brilliant light and heart-stifling heat,
The scratchings on the surface of the rock,
Utterings, scriptions, bafflings of the spirit,

The bewildered eye reads nonsense in the dazzle;
In the black depth of the rock the river says nothing,
Reflectionless, swift, intent, purposeless, flowing.

I said how beautiful is the past, how few the implements,
and how carefully made

The Guest Ellen at the Supper for Street People

The unclean spirits cry out in the body
Or mind of the guest Ellen in a loud voice
Torment me not, and in the fury of her unclean
Hands beating the air in some kind of unending torment—
Nobody witnessing could possibly know the event
That cast upon her the spell of this enchantment.

Almost all the guests are under some kind of enchantment:
Of being poor day after day in the same body;
Of being witness still to some obscene event;
Of listening all the time to somebody's voice
Whispering in the ear things divine or unclean,
In the quotidian of unending torment.

One has to keep thinking there was some source of torment,
Something that happened someplace else, unclean.
One has to keep talking in a reasonable voice
About things done, say, by a father's body
To or upon the body of Ellen, in enchantment
Helpless, still by the unforgotten event

Enchanted, still in the old forgotten event
A prisoner of love, filthy Ellen in her torment,
Guest Ellen in the dining hall in her body,
Hands beating the air in her enchantment,
Sitting alone, gabbling in her garbled voice
The narrative of the spirits of the unclean.

She is wholly the possessed one of the unclean.
Maybe the spirits came from the river. The enchantment
Entered her, maybe, in the Northeast Kingdom. The torment,
A thing of the waters, gratuitous event,
Came up out of the waters and entered her body
And lived in her in torment and cried out in her voice.

It speaks itself over and over again in her voice,
Cursing maybe or not a familiar obscene event
Or only the pure event of original enchantment
From the birth of the river waters, the pure unclean
Rising from the source of things, in a figure of torment
Seeking out Ellen, finding its home in her poor body.

Her body witness is, so also is her voice,
Of torment coming from unknown event;
Unclean is the nature and name of the enchantment.

I was the one who said
her body witness is, so also is her voice

HORACE, *Odes* I.11

To Leuconoë

Don't be too eager to ask
What the gods have in mind for us,
What will become of you,
What will become of me,
What you can read in the cards,
Or spell out on the Ouija board.
It's better not to know.
Either Jupiter says
This coming winter is not
After all going to be
The last winter you have,
Or else Jupiter says
This winter that's coming soon,
Eating away the cliffs
Along the Tyrrhenian Sea,
Is going to be the final
Winter of all. Be mindful.
Take good care of your household.
The time we have is short.
Cut short your hopes for longer.
Now as I say these words,
Time has already fled
Backwards away—
Leuconoë—
Hold on to the day.

I said better not know too much too soon all about it

One Two Three Four Five

anger

Anger is what I don't know what to do with.
I know it was anger was the trouble that other time.
I don't know where the anger came from, that time,
Or where it was I was going on anger's back
On a mission to somewhere to get me through the danger.

whatever

Whatever it is I think I probably know.
However whatever it is I keep from knowing.
No, it is not whatever I think I know.
Maybe I'll never know whatever it is.
Some day it has to be figured out. Whatever.

somebody

Somebody's got to tell me the truth some day.
And if somebody doesn't tell me the truth I'll tell it.
On my block there was somebody knew the truth, I think.
Or so I thought. Anyway somebody knew
That trying to tell the truth is looking for somebody.

isn't

If it isn't anywhere I guess it isn't.
But if it isn't why do I think it is?
I guess there really isn't any way
For me to find out what is or isn't there
In the black night where it either was or wasn't.

where

Where was it I was looking in the past?
It isn't where I've looked, that's no surprise.
I don't know what or where it is or was.
But maybe it isn't so much the where but the why.
Or maybe I haven't found it because beware.

where rhymes with beware, I said

Goodnight

Lying in bed and waiting to find out
Whatever is going to happen: the window shade

Making its slightest sound as the night wind,
Outside, in the night, breathes quietly on it;

It is parental hovering over the infantile;
Something like that; it is like being a baby,

And over the sleep of the baby there is a father,
Or mother, breathing, hovering; the streetlight light

In the nighttime branches breathing quietly too;
Altering; realtering; it is the body breathing;

The crib of knowing: something about what the day
Will bring; and something about what the night will hold,

Safely, at least for the rest of the night, I pray.

I said it is the body breathing,
the crib of knowing

Name

I wish I could recall now the lines written across the surface of my dream.
They said Name investigated the possibility of its own
happiness muttering and frowning preoccupied so that it noticed
nobody else at all though somehow you could tell that it knew somebody
was standing there in the doorway looking in at it and watching
what it was doing rummaging in desk drawers opening notebooks shutting
them up again writing down something or other on a scrap of paper
which would very soon be carelessly thrown away in a wastebasket and
go off in the trash somewhere out of the city burning stinking
unrecoverable although not biodegradable.

I wish I could recall now the lines written across my dream is what
I said

Horses

— for Tom Sleigh

It is true that, as he said, the horses,
When the lightning signaled something
Along the horizon, acknowledged the signaling,

Moving about in extraordinary beauty
Of shifting and neighing, flicker of ear,
Changings of pace, slidings, turnings,

The delicate legs finding out something
The ground could tell them, interpreting
The sky's statement of oncoming darkness.

The storm was doing whatever it does,
Matrix of signaling, along the horizon.
In the valley the houses were brilliantly

Clear, the storm's darkness was making
Possible a perfect delineation,
The houses' edges brimming with light.

I said the horse's hooves know all about it, the sky's statement of oncoming darkness

Roof

Four or five men on the high roof
Of the apartment house I see from out my window,

Angels or other beings from an element
Other than ours but similar although

Superior so bright and clear, perfected
In diminutive particular; angels

Or little brilliant demons or simian
Creatures with nose-and-mouth mask snouts

Against the fumes of the material
A tiny glittering machine is putting down.

The fumes are visible and drift away,
Like martyred souls made visible in the radiant air.

The fumes on the roof are visible and drifting away like
martyred souls, I said

Committee

Coldly the sun shone down on the moonlit scene.
Our committee stirred uneasily in its sleep.
Better not know too much too soon all about it.
The knees of grammar and syntax touched each other,
Furtive in pleasure under the oaken table.

The river lay not moving under the light
Of the shadowy earthly winter lunar scene.
The ends of justice are determined in
The conditions of our sleep. The spellbound scene
Arranged itself in a traditional way,

Transfixed and perfectly still. Unspoken agreements
Spoke volumes on the bookshelves of the room.

I said the knees of the committee touch each other under the table, furtive in pleasure

Graveyard

A writing I can't read myself: the picture
Of my father, taken a couple of years
Before he died; he is sitting alone some place
I don't know; maybe one of the meetings
He took to going to, trying to keep
His place in the world; he is smiling a little,
Cigarette smoke drifting away; he looks
Courteous, as always, not easy to know.

The side of a hill, nothing but a place;
Grass, dirt, a few scattered sticks, some stones,
The shadow of a tree; *Eurydice,*
My father; speaking the words as they are spoken
The meaning closes itself up; a manuscript
Written in a language only the dead speak.

I said

Eurydice, My Father

Out in the Cold

The sun shines in the ice of my country
As my smile glitters in the mirror of my devotion.
Flat is the scene there. There are a few scrub bushes.
I live on the edge of the land. The frozen sea
Lies locked for a thousand miles to the North, to the Pole.

Meager my mouth, and my knuckles sharp and white.
They will hurt when I hit. I fish for a fish
So thin and sharp in the tooth as to suit my malice.
It stares like any fish. But it knows a lot,
Knows what I know. Astonishment it has not.

I have a hut to which I go at night.
Sometimes there is no night, and the midnight sun
And I sit up all night and fish for that fish.
We huddle over the ice, the two of us.

I said we huddle over the ice,
the two of us

Poems of Marianne Moore

I

Let her look at a stone:
The stone becomes an apple,
The apple of her eye.

Nor is it only the stone:
Her eye becomes a hand
To hold the apple up,

Gently for the mind,
Which is the truest eye,
Kindly to look upon.

II

To squeeze from a stone its juice,
And find how sweet it is,
Is her art's happiness.

To squeeze from a stone its juice is her art's happiness is
what I said

Musings of Mind and Body

the mind

I am that thing the sea cast up, a shell
Within whose murmuring round the tide or wind
Murmur their old music. My coil is cunning,

Envy, malice, pity, contemplation ...
The wave that cast me out upon this beach
An hour ago, where I sit singing alone,

Will lace me round with her green arms, come tide,
Come evening, and I will be gone. Meanwhile
I hum to myself myself in a humming dream.

the body

I am that sea. What I cast up is mine,
Whenever I choose to take it back or not.
The driest bloom that spreads its papery petal

Far inland bears my legend on its flowering.
Read my sign in the lizard's grin. My voice
Cries out in the falling flesh of the great Bathsheba.

The little dog that leaps up in the field
Leaps up as if to leap out of my reach.
But I will wash him down. And thou, my mind.

I am the one who said,
I hum to myself myself in a humming dream

About Sylvia's Stories and Teaching

What's being taught
Is how language is seeing,
Telling, exacting.

And how we're caught
In language: in being,
In feeling, in acting.

And how we're caught, I said,
In language: in being, in feeling, in acting. I said, it's
exacting

On the Way to the Island

After we fled away from the shuddering dock,
The sea upheld us, would not let us go

Nor drown us, and we danced all night in the dark,
Till we woke to discover the deck was made of glass,

All glass, and, leaning together, we lovers looked down,
Say a hundred miles, say a million years, and there

Were the fish, huge, mouthing, motionless, flashing
Their innocent frightening scales in the dark!

I said the sea upheld us, would not let us go nor drown us,
and we looked down say a million years, and there were the
fish

Sculptures by Dimitri Hadzi

This metal blooms in the dark of Rome's
Day light. Of how many deaths
Is Rome the bright flowering?
See, the dead bloom in the dark
Of the Fosse Ardeatina. The black
Breath of the war has breathed on them:
Shields gleam, and helmets, in the memory.

Their flowering is their being true
To their own nature; not being
A glory, a victory; being a record,
The way things are in war.
In the nature of things the flowers grow
With the authority of telling the truth:
Their brightness is dark with it.

See, the dead bloom in the dark, I said

Caprimulgidae

Though *Caprimulgus* can only totter or hop
A few steps at a time, almost a cripple,
Nevertheless, perhaps on a flat roof
Of some city building or out on the bare ground,
Or catlike lengthwise stretched along a limb,
It lies all day, waking in its sleeping,
Capable, safe, concealed in its cryptic plumage,
Invisible to almost anything;
Its nightready eyes are closed, carefully
Keeping the brilliant secret of its flight;
Its hunting begins when the light begins to go.

It makes its flight in the competence of its own
Way of behaving; hovering, or gliding,
Floating, oddly, just at the edges of bushes,
Just over the ground, or near the vagueness of trees,
At twilight, on the hunt for moths or other
Creatures out in the failing evening light.
It feeds while flying softly, smiling, smiling,
The gape open to far back under the ears;
In the dim air it looks like a giant moth
Fluttering, the blurred disheveled feathers waving,
Signaling something that understands its meaning.

The nightjar feeds while flying softly, smiling, smiling, I said

HORACE, *Odes* I.4

To Sestius

Now the hard winter is breaking up with the welcome coming
Of spring and the spring winds; some fishermen,
Under a sky that looks changed, are hauling their caulked boats
Down to the water; in the winter stables the cattle
Are restless; so is the farmer sitting in front of his fire;
They want to be out of doors in field or pasture;
The frost is gone from the meadowgrass in the early mornings.
Maybe, somewhere, the nymphs and graces are dancing,
Under the moon the goddess Venus and her dancers;
Somewhere far in the depth of a cloudless sky
Vulcan is getting ready the storms of the coming summer.
Now is the time to garland your shining hair
With myrtle and with the flowers the free-giving earth has given;
Now is the right time to offer the kid or lamb
In sacrifice to Faunus in the firelit shadowy grove.

Revenant white-faced Death is walking not knowing whether
He's going to knock at a rich man's door or a poor man's.
O goodlooking fortunate Sestius, don't put your hope in the future;
The night is falling; the shades are gathering around;
The walls of Pluto's shadowy house are closing you in.
There who will be lord of the feast? What will it matter,
What will it matter there, whether you fell in love
With Lycidas, This or that girl with him, or he with her?

I said revenant whitefaced Death is walking not knowing whether

Rereading Old Writing

Looking back, the language scribbles.
What's hidden, having been said?
Almost everything? Thrilling to think
There was a secret there somewhere,
A bird singing in the heart's forest.

Two people sitting by a river;
Sunlight, shadow, some pretty trees;
Death dappling in the flowing water;
Beautiful to think about,
Romance inscrutable as music.

Out of the ground, in New Jersey, my mother's
Voice, toneless, wailing—beseeching?
Crying out nothing? A winter vapor,
Out of the urn, rising in the yellow
Air, an ashy smear on the page.

The quiet room floats on the waters,
Buoyed up gently on the daylight;
The branch I can see stirs a little;
Nothing to think about; writing
Is a way of being happy.

What's going to be in this place?
A person entering a room?
Saying something? Signaling?
Writing a formula on a blackboard.
Something not to be understood.

I said the formula on the blackboard said who are you

Gilgamesh (Tablet X)

"You who were born the son of a goddess mother,
why do you grieve because of a mortal father?

How long does a building stand before it falls?
How long does a contract last? How long will brothers

share the inheritance before they quarrel?
How long does hatred, for that matter, last?

Time after time the river has risen and flooded.
The insect leaves the cocoon to live but a minute.

How long is the eye able to look at the sun?
From the very beginning nothing at all has lasted.

See how the dead and the sleeping resemble each other.
Seen together, they are the image of death.

The simple man and the ruler resemble each other.
The face of the one will darken like that of the other.

The Annunaki gathered in assembly;
Mammetum, Mother Goddess, she was with them.

There they established that there is life and death.
The day of death is set, though not made known."

I said Utnapishtim said to Gilgamesh blink of an eye

The White Skunk

That glorious morning late in August when
The rosy-fingered dawn had scattered shadows
Away from the dreams I had dreamed the night before,
I looked out the back door of my condo, seeing
The parking lot we share, the cars we own,
And the houses all around, an embracing scene,
And there was Manfred and his small child Julia,
And, I thought for a moment, a little white toy
Trundling along behind her on its wheels.
But something was wrong with this. Julia, though little,
Wasn't so little as to be trundling such
A toy as what I thought I was seeing there,
On that glorious morning late in August when
The rosy-fingered dawn had scattered shadows.

And then I saw that the toy I thought I saw
Was not a toy but a little white skunk intently
Following Julia's legs and studying them,
And then, of course, her father had snatched her up
Into his arms, and was backing away from the skunk,
And kicking at it to get it away, but the skunk
Kept following, it seemed for a very long time,
As the three of them kept on this way on their way,
Julia crying now, a piercing cry,
And Manfred perplexed, a father protecting his child,
Backing away and saying, in a voice
Carefully calm and maybe pretending to be
Almost amused, "What should I do about this?"
Holding his child in his arms, having to keep
Backing away, unable to turn his back
On this bizarre studious creature following them.
Transfixed in the doorway of the place I live in
I stood there out of time, watching them go.

But then, as they were halfway down the driveway
The creature turned aside and disappeared
Into the tall grass alongside the driveway,
And Manfred, carrying Julia, was able to turn
And quickly make his way away from there
To the preschool across the street from the end of the driveway.
A moment later the skunk appeared again
And ran across the lawn beside our house,

I said where are you now   Where are you Anne

Intently studying the ground, near-sighted
Creature reading the ground for information,
Moving about the yard between our house
And the kindred house next door, purposeful, wandering.
What was it trying to find? Where was it going?—
A reader of the ground as if it were.

The walls of the facility at Mount Auburn
Where she kept wandering the halls, reading blank walls
To see if there was an exit there, or maybe
A bulletin board telling her what to do,
Telling her how to be there, or where to be,
Or what she was trying to find, or where she was going,
Intently studying where it was she was.

The skunk was white where a skunk is normally black,
And striped black where it's normally striped white.
Was it transmogrified? Come up from down there
In the Underworld where it could have been changed like that?
It came back over across the lawn toward where
I was standing transfixed in the doorway of my dwelling,
Its eyes still intently studying the ground,
Close reader of the text whose narrative
Or whose instruction it was following.

Orpheus, I, stepped back in nameless fear,
As it looked as if the skunk was reading its way
Toward the back porch steps up into my condo,
Coming toward me as if it were coming home.
And then the skunk ran past my back porch steps
Reading the ground, paying no heed to me,
And disappeared in the ground cover we planted
To ornament the dooryard of our dwellings
In the world the strange white skunk had disappeared from.

*

WALLACE STEVENS

The Man on the Dump

Day creeps down. The moon is creeping up.
The sun is a corbeil of flowers the moon Blanche
Places there, a bouquet. Ho-ho ... The dump is full
Of images. Days pass like papers from a press.
The bouquets come here in the papers. So the sun,
And so the moon, both come, and the janitor's poems
Of every day, the wrapper on the can of pears,
The cat in the paper-bag, the corset, the box
From Esthonia: the tiger chest, for tea.

The freshness of night has been fresh a long time.
The freshness of morning, the blowing of day, one says
That it puffs as Cornelius Nepos reads, it puffs
More than, less than or it puffs like this or that.
The green smacks in the eye, the dew in the green
Smacks like fresh water in a can, like the sea
On a cocoanut–how many men have copied dew
For buttons, how many women have covered themselves
With dew, dew dresses, stones and chains of dew, heads
Of the floweriest flowers dewed with the dewiest dew.
One grows to hate these things except on the dump.

Now, in the time of spring (azaleas, trilliums,
Myrtle, viburnums, daffodils, blue phlox),
Between that disgust and this, between the things
That are on the dump (azaleas and so on)
And those that will be (azaleas and so on),
One feels the purifying change. One rejects
The trash.

That's the moment when the moon creeps up
To the bubbling of bassoons. That's the time
One looks at the elephant-colorings of tires.
Everything is shed; and the moon comes up as the moon
(All its images are in the dump) and you see
As a man (not like an image of a man),
You see the moon rise in the empty sky.

Stanza my stone my father poet said

One sits and beats an old tin can, lard pail.
One beats and beats for that which one believes.
That's what one wants to get near. Could it after all
Be merely oneself, as superior as the ear
To a crow's voice? Did the nightingale torture the ear,
Peck the heart and scratch the mind? And does the ear
Solace itself in peevish birds? Is it peace,
Is it a philosopher's honeymoon, one finds
On the dump? Is it to sit among mattresses of the dead,
Bottles, pots, shoes and grass and murmur *aptest eve*:
Is it to hear the blatter of grackles and say
Invisible priest; is it to eject, to pull
The day to pieces and cry *stanza my stone*?
Where was it one first heard of the truth? The the.

*

An Alphabet

ABC
You and me

DEF
Dumb and deaf

GHI
Blind of eye

JKL
What's to tell?

MNO
All you know

PQR
Who you are

STU
Who are you?

VWX
Stones and sticks

YZ
You and me

vwx stones and sticks

October

The day was hot, and entirely breathless, so
The remarkably quiet remarkably steady leaf fall
Seemed as if it had no cause at all.

The ticking sound of falling leaves was like
The ticking sound of gentle rainfall as
They gently fell on leaves already fallen,

Or as, when as they passed them in their falling,
Now and again it happened that one of them touched
One or another leaf as yet not falling,

Still clinging to the idea of being summer:
As if the leaves that were falling, but not the day,
Had read, and understood, the calendar.

The day doesn't know what day it is, I said

Garden Dog

In the winter, out in the winter
Sunlight, watched from the upstairs

Window by the binocular eye,
Out in the winter light

The dog is wandering, sniffing
For enemies burrowed in Ireland

Sometime in the nineteenth century.
What's in a dog's heart?

The terrier brown coat
Touched into orange flame,

Blue, purple, pink,
By the binocular gaze,

The brilliant monster is wandering,
Smelling the winter air.

The wind is light. The light
Is wandering, blown by the breezes.

What's in the way the sun shines down?
Sniffing the sticks and stones,

Sniffing the dirt and dormant
Unflourishing grass in the garden,

Out in the winter light.

What's in the way the sun shines down, I said

At a Bar

While in a bar I bore
Indignity with those
Others whose hearts were sore
Or sour or sick or such
As made them humankind,
I looked into my glass
To see if I could find
Something to give me ease.

Narcissus at the pool,
I looked lovingly at
My own disordered fool,
Who would not tell me much.
But stared patiently back.
He would not tell me what
I'd ever have or lack
He would not tell me that.

I looked along the bar
And saw my fellow creature
Bravely standing there.
"By word, sign, or touch,"
I cried, in my mute heart,
"Tell me, be my teacher,
Be learnèd in that art,
What is my name and nature?"

My pulse ticked in my wrist;
The noon hung around unawares;
Outside the traffic passed.
Like quiet cattle or such,
Standing about a pool,
Dumb ignorant creatures,
My fellow, my self, my fool,
Ignorant of our natures.

I cried in my mute heart,
What is my name and nature

AFTERWORD

David Ferry has described his extraordinary poem, "Some Things I Said," as a "table of contents," and entertained the notion of expanding the number of stanzas to include fragments from all of his poems as well as one selection from each of his books of translation. As it stands, the entire arc of his work, and the essence of its content, may very well have taken shape in that exacting, visionary abruptness with which the poem crystallizes what his poetry can do, as one by one the cascade of lyric fragments demonstrates the enormous tonal range and cumulative power of his uncanny imagination. Above all his tender, grievously purified, eloquent recognition that we are all fellow sufferers, as inscrutable to ourselves as we are to others ("I cried in my mute heart, / What is my name and nature"). As such, bewildered creatures that we are, we often don't have the time of day—although how could we, since "The day doesn't know what day it is."

Perhaps most surprising is that the form of the poem does not allow the lines to assume an iambic pentameter structure—the art of the blank verse measure for which Richard Wilbur hailed David Ferry as the unrivaled contemporary master. There's great daring in this late, extensive break from a perfected, sovereign style. The subtitle of the poem, "writings on the wall" ("I wish I could recall now the lines written across my dream is what / I said") suggests a liminal, plainspoken oracular, urban graffiti. Writings on the darkening walls of Troy?

Encountering the jagged stanzas of "Some Things I Said," I cannot help hearing an echo akin to the fragmentary language of the songs in Virgil's penultimate eclogue, as we listen to the shepherds whose pastoral lyrics are breaking up in the dusky shadows of the sacred groves. "The shepherds trying to keep their world together in song replying to song replying to song," writes David Ferry, in one of his exquisite "Notes on Translation." "I was the one who said," sings the poet, as the lines break up yet the mournful eloquence remains.

—GEORGE KALOGERIS

ACKNOWLEDGMENTS AND SOURCES

I would like to thank my children Elizabeth and Stephen Ferry and my dear friend George Kalogeris for editing this book. I also want to thank my grandson Sebastian Wood and Victoria Sarria for editorial and design support, and Bella Bennett for proofreading and copy-editing. Diego Amaral, Alexandra Vergara, and Claudia Bedoya of Amaral Diseño lent their great expertise to the book's design. I am also grateful to my wonderful nieces, Judith, Sally and Susan Chaffee, for their careful, heartfelt reading. And to my great-niece Sara Langan for her help with our family's history, always an important source for my poetry.

I am very thankful to James Fraser, Ndidi Menkiti, and Carol Menkiti of the Grolier Poetry Press and Book Shop, and to the legacy of my friend and colleague Ifeanyi Menkiti, founder of the Grolier Press and owner of the Book Shop.

The poems in this volume are reprinted with permission from the following books and journals:

“To Sally,” in *Strangers.* Copyright 1983 by the University of Chicago Press. All rights reserved.

“Down by the River,” in *Of No Country I Know.* Copyright 1999 by the University of Chicago Press. All rights reserved. Previously published in *Harvard Magazine.*

“Poem,” in *Bewilderment.* Copyright 2012 by the University of Chicago Press. All rights reserved. Previously published in *Raritan.*

“News from Mount Amiata,” in *Of No Country I Know.* Copyright 1999 by the University of Chicago Press. All rights reserved. Previously published in *Raritan.*

“The Guest Ellen at the Supper for Street People,” in *Dwelling Places.* Copyright 1993 by the University of Chicago Press. Previously published in *Raritan.*

“To Leuconoë” Ode I. 11, in *The Odes of Horace*, translated by David Ferry. Copyright 1998 by Farrar, Straus and Giroux. All rights reserved.

“One Two Three Four Five,” in *Bewilderment.* Copyright 2012 by the University of Chicago Press. All rights reserved. Previously published in *Princetown Journal.*

“Goodnight,” in *Dwelling Places.* Copyright 1993 by the University of Chicago Press. All rights reserved. Previously published in *Boston Phoenix.*

“Name,” in *Dwelling Places.* Copyright 1993 by the University of Chicago Press. All rights reserved.

“Horses,” in *Dwelling Places.* Copyright 1993 by the University of Chicago Press. All rights reserved. Previously published in *Agni.*

“Roof,” in *Dwelling Places.* Copyright 1993 by the University of Chicago Press. All rights reserved.

“Committee,” in *Dwelling Places.* Copyright 1993 by the University of Chicago Press. All rights reserved.

“Graveyard,” in *Strangers.* Copyright 1983 by the University of Chicago Press. All rights reserved. Previously published in *The New Republic.*

“Out in the Cold,” in *On the Way to the Island.* Copyright 1960 by David Ferry. Published by Wesleyan University Press. Used by permission.

“Poems of Miss Marianne Moore*,” in *Of No Country I Know.* Copyright 1999 by the University of Chicago Press. All rights reserved. Previously published in *On the Way to the Island* as *“For the Birthday of Miss Marianne Moore, Whenever Her Birthday Is.”*

"Musings of Mind and Body," in *On the Way to the Island.* Copyright 1960 by David Ferry. Published by Wesleyan University Press. Used by permission.
"About Sylvia's Stories and Teaching," in *Of No Country I Know.* Copyright 1999 by the University of Chicago Press. All rights reserved.
"On the Way to the Island," in *On the Way to the Island.* Copyright 1960 by David Ferry. Published by Wesleyan University Press. Used by permission. Previously published in *New Poems by American Poets No. 2.*
"Sculptures by Dimitri Hadzi," in *Strangers.* Copyright 1983 by the University of Chicago Press. All rights reserved. Previously published in *Ploughshares.*
"Caprimulgidae," in *Strangers.* Copyright 1983 by the University of Chicago Press. All rights reserved. Previously published in *Poetry Miscellany.*
"To Sestius" Ode I. 4, in *The Odes of Horace*, translated by David Ferry. Copyright 1998 by Farrar, Straus and Giroux. All rights reserved.
Tablet X, in *Gilgamesh: A New Rendering in English Verse.* By David Ferry. Copyright 1993 by Farrar, Straus and Giroux. All rights reserved.
"The White Skunk," in *Bewilderment.* Copyright 2012 by the University of Chicago Press. All rights reserved. Previously published in *Slate.*
"The Man on the Dump," copyright 1923, 1951, 1954 by Wallace Stevens; from *The Collected Poems of Wallace Stevens* by Wallace Stevens. Used by permission of Alfred A. Knopf, an imprint of the Knopf Doubleday Publishing Group, a division of Penguin Random House LLC. All rights reserved.
"An Alphabet," in *Of No Country I Know.* Copyright 1999 by the University of Chicago Press. All rights reserved. Reprinted with permission.
"October," in *Bewilderment.* Copyright 2012 by the University of Chicago Press. All rights reserved. Previously published in *Daedalus.*
"Garden Dog," in *Dwelling Places.* Copyright 1993 by the University of Chicago Press. All rights reserved. Previously published in *Agni.*
"At a Bar," in *On the Way to the Island.* Copyright 1960 by David Ferry. Published by Wesleyan University Press. Used by permission. Previously published as *At A Low Bar.*